Presented To

_____

Date

_____

for
Fathers and Daughters

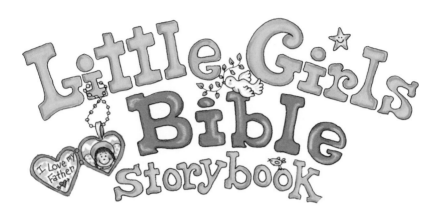

for
Fathers and Daughters

Carolyn Larsen
Illustrated by Caron Turk

BakerBooks

a division of Baker Publishing Group
Grand Rapids, Michigan

Text © 2000, 2014 by Carolyn Larsen
Illustrations © 2000 by Caron Turk

Published by Baker Books
a division of Baker Publishing Group
P.O. Box 6287, Grand Rapids, MI 49516-6287
www.bakerbooks.com

Printed in China

Library of Congress Cataloging-in-Publication Data
Larsen, Carolyn, 1950-
    Little girls Bible storybook for fathers and daughters / Carolyn Larsen; illustrated by Caron Turk.
        pages cm
    ISBN 978-0-8010-1549-6 (cloth)
    1. Bible stories, English. 2. Fathers and daughters—Religious aspects—Christianity—Juvenile literature. I. Turk, Caron, illustrator. II. Title.
BS551.3.L373 2014
220.95′05—dc23   2013025482

Scripture quotations are from God's Word®. © 1995 God's Word to the Nations. Used by permission of Baker Publishing Group.

14 15 16 17 18 19 20   7 6 5 4 3 2 1

Contents

Dear Dads,

The relationship a little girl has with her dad is so important. A good relationship helps establish a good self-image and self-confidence. Most little girls think their dads can do absolutely anything. Dad has a unique ability to teach his daughter the truths of the Bible and how to apply Scripture to life.

The Little Girls Bible Storybook for Fathers and Daughters *provides an opportunity to look at well-loved Bible stories through the eyes and hearts of the Bible characters who lived them. We don't really know how these people felt about the experiences they lived through. But they were people like we are, so we can imagine how they felt. By thinking about how these people may have felt, we can learn lessons of how to apply*

Scripture to our lives and how to make God real in every aspect of life.

Caron Turk has once again hidden a little angel in each illustration. I know that you and your little girl will have fun looking for this little angel. Hopefully, you'll be able to discuss the Bible story as you do your angel search. Caron and I pray that this book will provide hours of "together time" and entertainment with a purpose for you and your daughter. We pray that you will grow closer together and that both you and your daughter will go deeper in your relationship with the Lord through reading and talking about this book.

God bless,
Carolyn Larsen

Someone Like Me

Genesis 1–2

Plink, plink, plink, splash! Adam absentmindedly skipped rocks across a beautiful blue pond. He didn't seem to notice the animals playing around him. Tired of the rock skipping, Adam leaned back against a tree and sighed.

"What's the matter?" God asked.

"I'm a little lonely," Adam said. He didn't mean to be disrespectful. After all, God had given him a beautiful garden to live in.

"You need someone to talk to—someone who is more like you than the animals are," God said.

"Right," Adam said. "But there isn't anyone here like me. So what do we do?"

"Why don't you take a nap while I work on this?" God said.

While Adam slept, God gently tugged a rib from Adam's side and used it to make a new person. She was like Adam, but not exactly. "Welcome, Eve. You will be Adam's wife," God said.

"Adam, wake up," God whispered. Adam opened his eyes and saw a woman with long, curly hair. She smiled shyly at him. "This is Eve," God said. "She will be your wife. I made you both to be a lot like me. I'd like you to take care of things here in the garden."

Adam took Eve's hand. He wasn't lonely anymore.

Becoming a Woman of God

*A woman of God is made
in God's image.*

God made people in his image. That means we are a lot like him. If we remember that all people are made in God's image, we will treat them with kindness and respect.

God made you to be exactly the way he wants you to be. Be happy with who you are and be thankful for the things you can do!

A Verse to Remember

So God created humans in his image.
In the image of God he created them.
He created them male and female.

Genesis 1:27

Win or Lose
by What You Choose

Genesis 3

Eve pulled a piece of fruit from the tree and took a bite. *It's good!* she thought. She didn't notice the snake slithering toward her.

"Why are you eating that fruit when you could be having the sweetest, juiciest fruit in the garden?" the snake hissed.

"Who are you? I've never seen you in the garden before," Eve said.

"Let's just say I'm a friend," he hissed again. "Want some really good fruit?"

"I've tasted all the fruit here—and it's all good," Eve answered.

"There's one fruit you've never tasted," the snake said.

"Only the fruit from the tree that God told us not to touch," Eve said.

"Eating it will make you more like God." The snake dangled the shiny fruit in Eve's face.

the serpent was a crafty beast.....

This was a sad day for Adam and Eve

More like God, Eve thought. *That sounds good.* She took a bite. "This *is* good! Adam, try this."

Adam recognized the fruit. "God said we would die if we even touched this tree."

But soon Adam was eating the fruit too. Right away, though, he knew they had done something very wrong.

The Lord God sent Adam and Eve from the garden...

God didn't hide his disappointment. "You have to leave this beautiful garden," he said.

"I'm sorry we disobeyed you," Adam whispered.

"Me too," Eve said softly. "I should have remembered how much you love us."

"I know," God said. "I will punish you, but I'll always love you—no matter what."

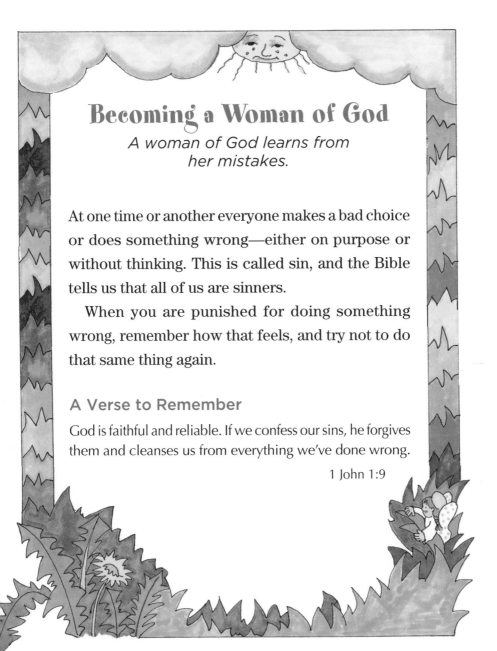

Becoming a Woman of God

A woman of God learns from her mistakes.

At one time or another everyone makes a bad choice or does something wrong—either on purpose or without thinking. This is called sin, and the Bible tells us that all of us are sinners.

When you are punished for doing something wrong, remember how that feels, and try not to do that same thing again.

A Verse to Remember

God is faithful and reliable. If we confess our sins, he forgives them and cleanses us from everything we've done wrong.

1 John 1:9

Houseboat Safety

Genesis 7–9

Mrs. Noah sighed. "I know God said to build this boat, but . . ."

"I know," Noah interrupted. "If people would just obey God, he wouldn't send a flood and we wouldn't be building this boat."

"And, all these animals wouldn't be coming," Mrs. Noah whispered.

As soon as the animals and Noah's family were inside the boat, it started to rain. *It's been raining for over a month,* Mrs. Noah thought one night. *The whole earth must be flooded by now.*

One morning Mrs. Noah noticed something was different. "The rain has stopped." Just as she said that, the boat bumped something.

"We've hit ground!" Noah shouted. He peeked out and saw that the boat was sitting on the very top of a big mountain. All around them was water.

Day after day Noah checked to see if the floodwaters were gone. Finally, one day he called, "I'm opening the door. We can leave the boat!"

Mrs. Noah shooed out the animals. Quickly sweeping the boat clean, she joined Noah on dry ground.

Noah and his family were the only people left on earth. The first thing they did was thank God for keeping them safe. Then Mrs. Noah noticed a colorful arch in the sky. "What is that?" she asked.

"It's a rainbow," God answered. "It shows my promise to never send a flood to destroy the whole earth again. Every time you see a rainbow, remember how much I love you."

Becoming a Woman of God

*A woman of God is thankful
for God's care.*

God kept Noah and his family safe because they loved and obeyed him. As soon as Mr. and Mrs. Noah stepped out of the boat, they thanked God for keeping them safe.

When we do something helpful for someone else, it feels nice being thanked, doesn't it? That's a good reminder to thank God for all he does for us.

A Verse to Remember

Give thanks to the LORD because he is good,
  because his mercy endures forever.

1 Chronicles 16:34

Choosing Your Way

Genesis 13

Lot's life was good. He owned herds of sheep and cattle, and had hundreds of men working for him.

Lot's uncle, Abram, had even more than Lot did. Both families had set up camp near the Jordan River.

"Hey, get your sheep out of here. We got here first!" Lot's shepherds shouted. They tried to shove Abram's sheep out of the way. Pretty soon the two groups of shepherds were pushing each other and shouting.

Abram heard the arguing. *This isn't right*, he thought; *someone is going to get hurt if this fighting doesn't stop.* So he went to see his nephew. "Let's stop fighting. We have all this land around us. Why don't we go our separate ways? Then there will be plenty of food and water for our animals," he said.

"You're right," Lot agreed. He looked around at the wide open countryside. The land around the Jordan River looked like a garden. There would be plenty of food there for his animals. He knew that the land farther away was more like a desert. It would be harder to find food and water there.

"I'll stay here," Lot announced.

Abram packed up his tent and moved his animals and his family away from the Jordan River. "Abram," God said, "look around you. I'm going to give all this land to you someday. You will have as many children as there are stars in the sky. I'm going to bless you, Abram."

Becoming a Woman of God
A woman of God seeks peace.

Abram could have argued with Lot because Lot wanted the best land, but he didn't. He thought it was more important to have peace. It was an example of God's love. He knew that God would take care of him.

How good are you at living peacefully with other people? Do you always want to have your own way?

A Verse to Remember

Accept my encouragement. Share the same attitude and live in peace. The God of love and peace will be with you.

2 Corinthians 13:11

A Baby Named Laughter

Genesis 18:1–15; 21:1–7

Sarah was busy cooking a special dinner. Her husband, Abraham, was outside talking with three men who had dropped by. Sarah didn't know them, but a good hostess always offered travelers a meal. Sarah heard one of the strangers say something that surprised her.

Sarah laughed so hard she dropped a spoon. "That man thinks I'm going to have a baby! Me—with my gray hair, bad eyesight, and wrinkled skin? I'm too old to have a baby."

The men sitting outside with Abraham looked toward the tent. "Why did Sarah laugh at our news?" they asked. "God is the one giving you this baby. Is anything too hard for God?" Abraham didn't know what to say. God had promised them a family a long time ago. But now he and Sarah were so old; it just didn't make any sense.

A few months later Sarah wasn't laughing anymore. Each time she felt the baby move inside her, she was amazed. "Put your hand here," she said, grabbing Abraham's hand. She laid it on her bulging tummy and smiled as the baby kicked against it.

When their son was born, Abraham and Sarah named him Isaac, which means laughter. Sarah wrapped Isaac in a soft blanket and rocked him gently. "Your father and I have quite a story to tell you," she whispered. "You are a precious gift from God."

Becoming a Woman of God

A woman of God trusts his promises.

God promised to give Abraham and Sarah a big family. They waited a long time for their first child. Sometimes we have to wait a long time for promises to be kept. Waiting teaches us to trust God even more.

When was a time you had to wait awhile for someone to keep their promise to you?

A Verse to Remember

We must continue to hold firmly to our declaration of faith. The one who made the promise is faithful.

Hebrews 10:23

Moving On

Genesis 37, 39–45

"Joseph always thinks he's right," one of Joseph's brothers grumbled.

"Yeah, and Dad likes Joseph best. Just look at that fancy coat he gave him. None of us have anything like that," another one said.

One day all the brothers were out in the field. "Hey," one brother said, "look at those men coming this way. Let's sell Joseph to them to be a slave and just tell Dad that a wild animal ate him."

Next thing Joseph knew, he was a slave in Egypt. Then someone lied about him and he landed in jail. He could have been angry with God, but he wasn't. Instead his faith grew stronger.

A couple of years later, the pharaoh of Egypt had dreams he couldn't understand. "A prisoner named Joseph can explain dreams," someone told him. Joseph explained the pharaoh's dreams. Pharaoh was so happy that he made Joseph second in command in the land.

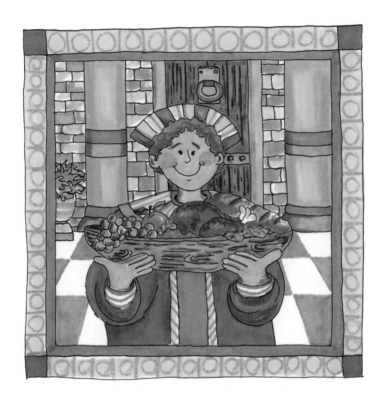

Then there was a drought in the land; people had no food to eat. Things were tough—except in Egypt where Joseph had stored water and food. People came from everywhere to buy food from him. One day his brothers came, but they didn't recognize him. Joseph knew that the right thing to do was to forgive his brothers. He gave them food and brought them to live with him in Egypt.

Becoming a Woman of God
A woman of God forgives others.

If anyone ever had a reason to be angry with someone, Joseph did. His brothers did a terrible thing by selling him into slavery. But what good would it do for Joseph to keep holding a grudge against them?

God forgives us for wrong things we do, so we should forgive others when they hurt us.

A Verse to Remember

Everyone will know that you are my disciples because of your love for each other.

John 13:35

Where There's a Will, There's a Way

Exodus 2:1-10

"Momma, what if Pharaoh's soldiers find our baby? What will they do to him?" Miriam asked Jochebed. She had heard their neighbors talking about Pharaoh's orders to get rid of all the Hebrew baby boys. Now that she had a baby brother, she was frightened.

"I don't care what Pharaoh ordered," Jochebed said as she hugged Moses tightly. "I have a plan to keep Baby Moses safe. But I need your help, Miriam." The big sister was happy to do whatever she could. Jochebed put Moses in Miriam's arms and said, "Try to keep him quiet."

Jochebed hurried to the river and picked some grass reeds. Walking home, she tried not to draw attention to herself. Once she was safely inside her house, she wove the reeds into a small basket.

After she and Miriam went back to the river, Jochebed drew Moses close and kissed the top of his head. "Take care of this boy, God," Jochebed prayed as she tucked Moses into the little basket.

"Momma, here's his blanket," Miriam whispered. She trusted her mom to do what was best for Moses.

Miriam hid by the river, watching. When a princess opened the basket and picked up Moses, Miriam knew everything was going to be all right. A few minutes later she ran home. "Momma, come quick! Pharaoh's daughter found Moses. She's going to keep him, but she wants a Hebrew to take care of him."

"Praise God," Jochebed prayed.

Becoming a Woman of God

A woman of God does what she can.

Moms and dads will do just about anything they can to take care of their children. Jochebed took quite a chance by keeping Moses hidden, but she did what she could to keep him safe.

Jochebed asked for God's direction, then got busy. We should follow her example.

A Verse to Remember

Whoever speaks must speak God's words. Whoever serves must serve with the strength God supplies so that in every way God receives glory through Jesus Christ. Glory and power belong to Jesus Christ forever and ever! Amen.

1 Peter 4:11

No Need for Water Wings

Exodus 11:1–15:21

Miriam hugged her daughter. When Moses told her that something terrible was going to happen to the Egyptians, Miriam was sad.

Why didn't Pharaoh just listen to God? she thought. *God just wanted him to let us leave Egypt.*

That night things happened just as God said they would. The oldest child in every Egyptian home died. Finally, after this tenth plague, Pharaoh begged the Israelites to leave.

The people going watched the pillar of fire at night and the column of smoke in the daytime. "God is with us; he's leading us," they said. Finally, they set up camp on the shore of the Red Sea. Miriam was glad to rest awhile. But then she heard someone shout, "Pharaoh's army is chasing us!" *Oh no; what will Moses do now?* Miriam wondered.

Moses climbed up on a rock. "Watch what God will do for you!" he said. Then the waters began to part into two big walls—with a dry pathway in the middle.

Miriam followed the other Israelites through the Red
Sea. Every single Israelite crossed safely. "The Egyptians
are following us into the sea," someone shouted. Just
then, the water walls rolled together, and every Egyptian died. "We're safe!" Miriam said as she grabbed a
tambourine and joined her friends in praising God.

Becoming a Woman of God

A woman of God knows God is in control.

God sent nine plagues, but Pharaoh still wouldn't let the Israelites go. The tenth plague—the death of the oldest child in each Egyptian home—convinced Pharaoh to let the Israelites go. But when the Egyptians started chasing them, some of the Israelites thought God might have lost control of the situation.

God always takes care of us. Seeing his plan unfold helps our trust and confidence in him grow.

A Verse to Remember

Never worry about anything. But in every situation let God know what you need in prayers and requests while giving thanks.

Philippians 4:6

Add One Branch and Stir Gently

Exodus 15:22–25

Moses was a man on a mission—leading the Israelites to the land God had promised to them. He didn't have time to look back at the Red Sea. Soon a long parade of people was marching toward the desert.

"Moses, the people are thirsty. You've got to find water for them." Miriam was elected the spokesperson, since Moses was her brother.

"We're in a desert; where would I find water?" Moses said. It seemed to him like the people complained about everything, forgetting all that God had done to free them from slavery.

Moses led his people farther into the desert. They walked for three days with no water and complained every step of the way. Finally, at Marah they found a pool of water. They crowded around and began scooping the water into their mouths.

"Yuck! This water is bitter. We can't drink it. What are you going to do about this?" they shouted at Moses. "God, help me. The people are angry," Moses cried.

"Pick up that branch and throw it in the water," God answered. Moses saw the branch beside a rock. With a mighty heave he tossed it into the pool of bitter water.

Then, one brave woman dipped her finger in for a taste. "It's sweet now. Drink up everyone."

Becoming a Woman of God

A woman of God turns to God for help.

Moses was leading the people to the Promised Land. When the people got angry, they focused their anger on Moses. He may have wanted to run far away from the Israelites, but he had a job to do and he was going to do it. So he prayed for God's help, and God helped him.

A Verse to Remember

Turn all your anxiety over to God because he cares for you.

1 Peter 5:7

A Teamwork Victory

Exodus 17:8–16

"Joshua," Moses called. "We have a problem. There are some soldiers hiding over there, and they don't look too friendly."

"That's because they are Amalekites—our worst enemies," Joshua said.

"Call your soldiers," Moses commanded.

The next morning Moses stood on a big hill and held his arms out wide with his shepherd's staff pointing to heaven. Joshua's army fought hard. Even though the Amalekite army was bigger and stronger, Joshua's soldiers were winning.

"Oh, my arms," Moses moaned. "It feels like my staff weighs 500 pounds." His arms slowly dropped down to his sides—but when they did, the Amalekites started winning. It seemed like Joshua's soldiers couldn't do anything right.

"Help me," Moses said. Aaron and Hur ran to Moses and stood on either side of him. They held his arms high in the air, and Joshua's army won. They beat the bigger, stronger Amalekites.

"We won!" The soldiers shouted and celebrated as the
Amalekites ran away. Moses celebrated too. He built an
altar and named it "The Lord is my banner," and all the
Israelites thanked God for his help.

Becoming a Woman of God

A woman of God is part of a team.

Joshua's army would have lost the battle if Moses hadn't held his staff up. It was a sign that God was with them. And Moses wouldn't have been able to hold his staff up until the battle was over if Aaron and Hur hadn't helped him. Winning this battle was a team effort.

Have you ever been part of a team? It feels good to work with others to obey God and accomplish a goal.

A Verse to Remember

Two people are better than one because together they have a good reward for their hard work.

Ecclesiastes 4:9

Ten Simple Rules

Exodus 18:5; 19:1–20:21

"Ever since we left Egypt, we have walked. Are we ever going to get where we're going?" Moses's wife Zipporah wondered aloud. At least they had set up camp now. Mount Sinai rose into the sky right behind them.

After supper, Zipporah tumbled into bed. Moses came in. "God called me. I'm going up the mountain," he told her.

"Can't you wait until morning? You must be even more tired than I am," Zipporah said. She knew Moses was responsible for the Israelites, but she worried about him.

When Moses came down the mountain he announced, "God wants to speak to everyone." A few days later, the Israelites stood together at the foot of the mountain. Thunder crashed all around them, and lightning flashed across the sky. Zipporah could barely catch her breath.

Being in the presence of the awesome God was frightening. Zipporah had new respect for her husband, who was often called into God's presence. She looked up to see Moses climbing the mountain once again, disappearing into the clouds for a meeting with God.

Moses was gone for a long time. Zipporah began to wonder if she would ever see him again.

When Moses finally came back he was carrying two huge stone tablets. "God himself wrote these ten rules for us to live by," Moses told the people. "They tell us how to treat God and each other."

Becoming a Woman of God

A woman of God understands that rules are to help her live correctly.

God gave the Ten Commandments to the Israelites to make their lives easier. Does that sound backwards? Some people think that rules make our lives harder, but that isn't really true. When we have rules to go by, we know what is expected of us.

The Ten Commandments are for us today too. They teach us the right way to honor and respect God and how to treat other people.

A Verse to Remember

Those who obey Christ's commandments live in God, and God lives in them. We know that he lives in us because he has given us the Spirit.

1 John 3:24

Grapeland

Numbers 13–14

"You twelve spies will go into Canaan," Moses announced. "Here are your instructions: God wants you to see if good crops grow there, if the towns have walls, and if the armies are big."

Once in the land the spies looked around. "Look at the size of those grapes!" one man whispered. "Let's cut a cluster and take it back to show everyone."

Forty days later, the twelve men returned to Moses and reported what they had found. "Wonderful crops grow in Canaan—just look at these huge grapes. It's a beautiful land, with plenty of food and water."

"But the people there are giants! And the cities have big walls around them," another man said.

The spies argued among themselves about whether the Israelites should try to capture the land. Two spies, Joshua and Caleb, said, "Let's go for it. God already said that the land is ours." But the other ten were afraid of the giants.

The whole crowd sided with the ten who were afraid. Caleb and Joshua were frustrated.

God was even more frustrated than Caleb and Joshua. "I told you that I was giving you the land. Since you don't believe me, you will wander around for forty years. After that I'll give your people this land but none of you will be alive to see it except Caleb and Joshua, who believed me."

Becoming a Woman of God

A woman of God believes God.

God had already told the Israelites that he was going to give them the land of Canaan. But they didn't trust him enough to believe he would help them defeat the giants who lived there or knock down the big walls around the cities.

The stories in the Bible remind us how awesome and powerful God is.

A Verse to Remember

Faith assures us of things we expect and convinces us of the existence of things we cannot see.

Hebrews 11:1

Showdown at the Old Oak Tree

Judges 6:1–24

"God, save us," the Israelite people prayed. They forgot that the reason they were having so many problems was because they kept disobeying God. "We've lost our homes, our cattle, our crops. We're starving!"

God heard their cries and sent an angel to sit beneath an old oak tree where Gideon was threshing wheat. "Mighty hero, the Lord is with you," the angel said.

"If God is with us, why are we having so many problems?" Gideon asked.

"God is sending you to rescue the people," the angel answered.

Gideon didn't know what to think about that. "Surely I'm not the best choice. I'm going to need some proof that God really wants me for this job," he said.

The angel waited patiently while Gideon hurried home to cook a goat and bake some bread. When he returned, the angel said, "Put the goat and bread on that rock over there and pour broth over them."

"Stand back," the angel said. He touched the dripping meat and bread with his staff, and fire shot out from the rock. Every drop of meat, bread, and gravy burned up. Now Gideon knew that God wanted him to do this job.

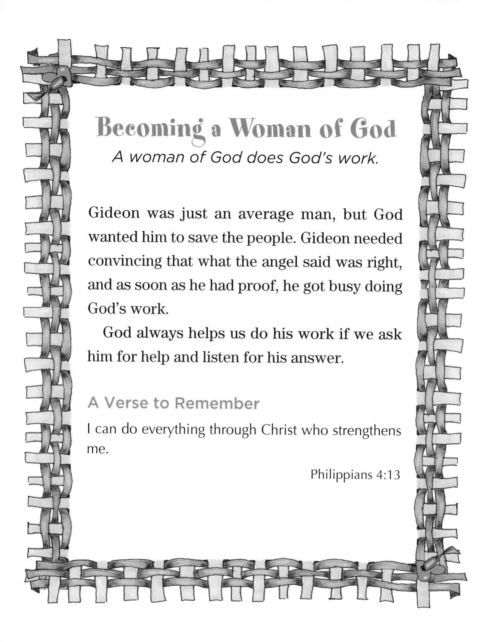

Becoming a Woman of God

A woman of God does God's work.

Gideon was just an average man, but God wanted him to save the people. Gideon needed convincing that what the angel said was right, and as soon as he had proof, he got busy doing God's work.

God always helps us do his work if we ask him for help and listen for his answer.

A Verse to Remember

I can do everything through Christ who strengthens me.

Philippians 4:13

Nighttime Obedience

Judges 6:25–32

"Gideon, I'm tired of Israel worshiping other gods. Help me put a stop to it. Tear down your father's altar to other gods. Build an altar to me in its place," God said.

"Everyone in town worships Baal. If I knock down their altar, they're going to be really mad," Gideon said.

But God did not change his request. So Gideon waited until everyone was sleeping. He ordered his servants, "Pull down this altar. Don't leave one stone in place."

When the altar was down, Gideon built an altar to God. Heaving a big bull onto it, he sacrificed it to God. "Father, thank you for loving us," he said. "Forgive your people once again for turning away from you."

The next morning people asked, "What happened to Baal's altar? Who did this?"

"Someone built a new altar and sacrificed a bull to God," one person said. Quickly a mob started looking for whoever had done this. The evidence pointed to Gideon, so they went to his house.

"Give us your son. He's going to pay for this!" the mob shouted at Gideon's father, Joash. "He wrecked Baal's altar!" Gideon hid behind a door and prayed.

Joash asked the people "Why are you fighting Baal's battle? If he's really so powerful, let him rebuild his own altar. We should be worshiping the real God instead of a fake one."

Becoming a Woman of God

A woman of God takes a stand for him.

Gideon took a stand for God when he knew that the rest of the people were not going to like it.

Have you ever stood up for something that you believed was right, even if your friends didn't agree with you? Were you glad that you did?

A Verse to Remember

Some have refused to let their faith guide their conscience and their faith has been destroyed like a wrecked ship.

1 Timothy 1:19

You're the One!

1 Samuel 16:1-13

"We're going to meet Samuel the priest, and you can't come," David's brother teased. "You're only good for taking care of the sheep. We older brothers have more important things to do."

He's only a little bit older than me, David thought. *I wish I could meet Samuel.* He turned around to see his father and all seven of his older brothers leaving for the meeting. Dragging his staff in the dirt, David headed for the field.

David settled down near his sheep. Meanwhile at the meeting in town, Samuel asked to meet David's older brothers. Eliab, the oldest, came to Samuel. He was tall and strong and very handsome. Samuel seemed excited to meet him, but after a few minutes of silence, he asked to meet the next boy.

Soon Samuel had met all of the boys. "The Lord hasn't chosen any of them," he said. "Jesse, do you have any other sons?"

"My youngest is at home watching the sheep. But why would you care about him?" Jesse answered.

Samuel said, "Go get him."

As soon as David came, Samuel ran to him and laid his hands on David's shoulders. "You're the one," he said. "God has told me that you will be king of Israel. I am here to anoint you." David was filled with joy as Samuel poured the anointing oil on his head.

Becoming a Woman of God

A woman of God may be a child.

David's older brothers thought that David wasn't worth much because he was the youngest. But God doesn't look at how big or strong we are. God looks at our hearts to see if we love him and want to serve him.

A Verse to Remember

Don't let anyone look down on you for being young. Instead, make your speech, behavior, love, faith, and purity an example for other believers.

1 Timothy 4:12

A Stone's Throw

1 Samuel 17:1–51

"You're always acting like such a big shot. Why don't you just go home?" Eliab shoved his little brother, and David tumbled to the ground.

"Father sent me here to bring this stuff to you guys," David tried to explain. "I was just looking around. I've never seen an army camp before."

"Why aren't any of King Saul's soldiers willing to fight that Philistine giant, Goliath?" David asked. Eliab didn't answer; he just stomped away.

Just then David heard Goliath shouting again, "Hey, Israelites; send someone out to fight me!"

David looked around at the big, strong soldiers. None of them would even look back at him. So David marched into King Saul's tent and said, "I'm just a kid, but I'll fight the giant."

King Saul looked at David, then he looked out at the giant Goliath. "OK, but at least wear my armor," he said. But when David put it on he couldn't walk because the armor was too heavy." So he took it off. "I'll do this my way with God's help," he said.

Hurrying down the hill, David stopped to pick up five stones. *Goliath, you can't win because God is helping me,* David thought. He calmly put a stone in his sling-shot and swung it around and around. The stone flew through the air and hit Goliath right in the head. The earth shook as the giant dropped to the ground. "David won!" King Saul's soldiers shouted.

Becoming a Woman of God

*A woman of God
fights in God's strength.*

David knew that he wouldn't have a chance against a giant soldier like Goliath unless God helped him. That was something King Saul's soldiers didn't understand, or one of them would have fought the giant.

When you have Christ living in your heart, you are never alone. He will help you with the tough things you may have to do, if you just ask him.

A Verse to Remember

Nothing is impossible for God.

Luke 1:37

Shhhh! Did You Hear Something?

1 Kings 19:8–18

King Ahab and Queen Jezebel were angry because they thought Elijah had killed 400 prophets of their god, Baal. Afraid for his life, Elijah ran away.

Elijah came to a cave near the top of Mount Sinai. "What are you doing here?" a voice asked.

It was God. "I've spent my life teaching about you," Elijah said. "But the people break their promises to you, tear down your altars, even kill your prophets. I'm the only one left!"

"Stand on the mountain," God commanded. Elijah crept outside the cave. Suddenly a strong wind began to blow until rocks pulled away from the mountain and tumbled down. Elijah held on for dear life. "God," he said, "was I supposed to hear your voice in this powerful wind?"

The earth began to move as if someone had picked up the mountain and was shaking it. Elijah fell to his knees and held on to a tree trunk. *Is God trying to speak to me now?* he wondered.

Then he looked up and saw a wall of fire roaring up the mountain. Dashing back into the cave, Elijah listened for God to speak, but he heard nothing.

When the fire passed, he heard a gentle whisper float-
ing up the mountain. It was the voice of God: "You aren't
alone, Elijah. There are still others who love me."

Becoming a Woman of God

A woman of God listens for his voice.

To hear God's voice, be in a quiet place for a while and listen. When God speaks, it won't be in a voice that sounds like a person; it's more like a whisper inside your heart.

Do you ever hear God's voice speaking inside your heart?

A Verse to Remember

Beauty is something internal that can't be destroyed. Beauty expresses itself in a gentle and quiet attitude which God considers precious.

1 Peter 3:4

The Great Oil Jar Adventure

2 Kings 4:1–7

"Momma, that man scares me," the little boy cried. His older brother was scared too. Their mom hugged the boys and watched the man walk away. *My boys are right*, she thought. *That man is mean.*

Of course, she would never say that out loud. But ever since her husband died, the mean man had been threatening her. He said her husband had owed him a lot of money and he wanted it *now*!

The woman hurried across town to see Elisha. The prophet of God listened as she blurted out her story. "My boys are all I have left. Please don't let him take them," she begged.

Elisha and the woman hurried to her house. "You have one jar of olive oil here, right?" he asked. She nodded. "Find as many empty jars as you can. Send your sons to borrow some from your neighbors," he ordered. The boys hurried from neighbor to neighbor.

"Pour oil into that first jar. Keep filling jars until your own jar is empty," Elisha said. The woman didn't question him. She started pouring oil.

She filled jar after jar from her one little jar. "Praise God; he's taking care of us."

Elisha smiled as he told the woman, "Sell this extra oil. Pay the man and keep whatever money is left over to buy food for your family."

Becoming a Woman of God

*A woman of God goes to someone
who can help.*

The woman certainly had a problem. She did exactly the right thing by going to someone who could help her.

Have you ever had a problem that you couldn't solve? Did you go to someone who could help you?

A Verse to Remember

God is our refuge and strength,
    an ever-present help in times of trouble.

Psalm 46:1

Home Sweet Home

2 Kings 4:8-11

Elisha came into Shunem tired and hungry. As he traveled from town to town, someone would invite him to stay at their home or come for dinner. In Shunem it always seemed to be the same kind woman.

She was a great cook and very generous with the nice home she and her husband shared. Elisha always looked forward to staying with her. Tonight this prophet of God needed a good rest.

The next morning Elisha continued on his journey. As the kind woman waved good-bye to him, an idea popped into her head. Later that night she shared her idea with her husband. "Why don't we add a room onto our house just for Elisha? Then he would have a place to stay anytime he comes to Shunem."

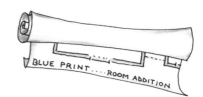

Her husband, who was just as generous as she was, thought her idea was a good one. Right away he started measuring and hammering and sawing. The room was ready and waiting the next time Elisha came to Shunem.

Thank You, God

A few weeks later Elisha returned, and everyone he greeted seemed to be keeping a secret. *I wonder what's going on here,* Elisha thought to himself. He soon found out as the kind woman and her husband showed Elisha the new room built just for him. Elisha praised God for their generosity.

Becoming a Woman of God

A woman of God is generous.

This woman was generous and kind. She didn't have to build a special room for Elisha, but she knew that whatever money she and her husband had was a gift from God, so she and her husband used that money to serve God. How do you show generosity to others?

A Verse to Remember

The whole group of believers lived in harmony. No one called any of his possessions his own. Instead, they shared everything.

Acts 4:32

Beauty *and* Bravery

Esther

Esther went from being a simple, beautiful Jewish girl to queen of Persia. Everyone loved Esther. She was kind and loving.

But Esther had a problem. "Haman ordered everyone to bow down to him, but I will only bow to God," Esther's relative Mordecai told her. "Now he wants to get rid of all the Jewish people."

"I can't help. No one—not even the king—knows that I am Jewish. You told me to keep it a secret," Esther said.

"I know. But perhaps God made you queen so you can save your people!"

That night Esther couldn't sleep. She wondered what would happen when the king found out that she was Jewish. Finally, early in the morning, she sent a note to Mordecai: "I'm going to talk to the king. Have all the Jews fast and pray for me."

Esther invited the king and Haman to a special banquet. The two men laughed and talked as they ate. But Esther was so nervous that she could barely speak. Finally, just before dessert she blurted out, "Haman is planning to get rid of me and all my people!"

The king listened as Esther explained Haman's plan
and revealed that she was Jewish. She was relieved
when the king called in his guards to lead Haman away.
The people were saved, thanks to the courage of the
beautiful young queen.

Becoming a Woman of God

*A woman of God asks others
to pray for her.*

Esther did what she could to stop Haman's plan. But before she went to the king she asked people to pray for her. She knew that in order to be able to save her people, she needed God's help.

Have you ever asked someone to pray for you? Did you feel better knowing that someone was praying for you?

A Verse to Remember

Pray in the Spirit in every situation. Use every kind of prayer and request there is. For the same reason be alert. Use every kind of effort and make every kind of request for all of God's people.

Ephesians 6:18

Broccoli Banquets

Daniel 1

"Steak and potatoes; this is the life," the guys around Daniel said as they leaned back on satin couches.

"Remember, we're slaves. We aren't free. Don't get caught up in the fancy food. It's offered to Babylon's idols before it's given to us. This is serious," Daniel said.

"You worry too much," one boy said. "You'd probably rather be in a jail cell instead of living in a palace!"

"Isn't anyone with me here?" Daniel asked. His friends, Shadrach, Meshach, and Abednego stepped forward. The four of them went off by themselves to hear Daniel's plan.

"My friends and I don't want this fancy food. Just give us vegetables and water," Daniel told one of the guards.

"No, you are being trained to serve in the king's palace. If you aren't as healthy as the other prisoners, I will be in trouble," the guard said.

"How about a ten-day test? Then if we aren't healthy, we'll eat your food," Daniel said. So for ten days the guard slipped Daniel and his friends vegetables and water while the other prisoners ate the king's food.

A wonderful thing happened; Daniel and his friends grew stronger and healthier than any of the others. "It's veggies and water for you from now on," the guard said.

At the end of the training the king was more impressed with Daniel, Shadrach, Meshach, and Abednego than anyone else.

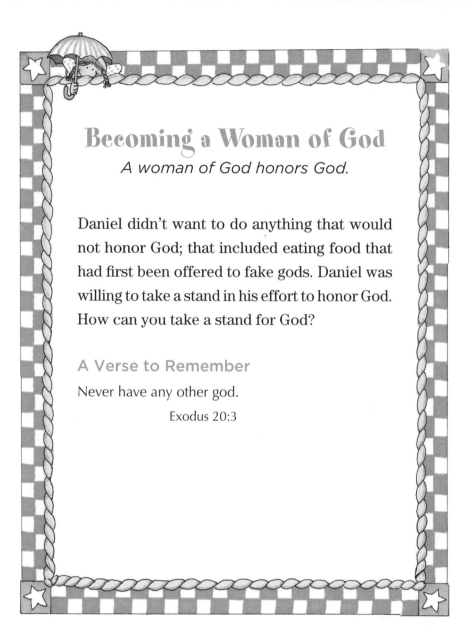

Becoming a Woman of God

A woman of God honors God.

Daniel didn't want to do anything that would not honor God; that included eating food that had first been offered to fake gods. Daniel was willing to take a stand in his effort to honor God. How can you take a stand for God?

A Verse to Remember

Never have any other god.

Exodus 20:3

The Birth of the King

Luke 2:1–20

If only we didn't have to go to Bethlehem to be counted in the census, Mary thought.

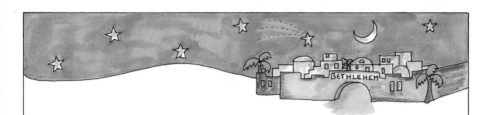

Joseph could have gone alone, but since her baby was due any day Mary didn't want to be away from him. "Are you OK, Mary?" Joseph asked.

She answered, "Yes. Is it much farther?"

"We'll be there soon, and we'll get a room with a soft bed so you can rest," Joseph promised.

Mary was surprised to see so many people in Bethlehem. They had come to be counted in the census. She waited while Joseph went to get a room. She couldn't wait to lie down.

"There aren't any rooms—the whole town is full. The innkeeper said that since you're pregnant, we can stay in his stable. I'm sorry," Joseph said.

"It's OK. I just want to lie down," Mary said with a sigh. She settled down on some clean straw and fell asleep. A few hours later, she woke up. "Joseph, the baby. *Wake up!*"

Joseph tried to help in any way he could. Finally he laid the newborn baby in Mary's arms.

Mary wrapped Jesus in a clean blanket and kissed him. Mary and Joseph watched in amazement as the baby slept. "He's the Son of God," Mary whispered.

"I know," Joseph said. "God trusts us to raise his Son. This little boy will grow up to be our Savior."

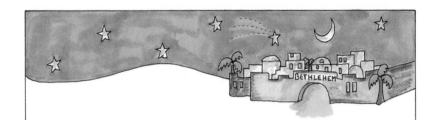

Becoming a Woman of God

A woman of God knows her Savior.

Mary knew Jesus in a way that no one else ever has. She was his earthly mother, but she knew that Jesus would be her Savior too.

Do you believe that Jesus is your Savior? Do you understand that you are a sinner and that Jesus died for your sins so you can live in heaven with him someday?

A Verse to Remember

My sheep respond to my voice, and I know who they are. They follow me, and I give them eternal life. They will never be lost, and no one will tear them away from me.

John 10:27–28

Night Run to Egypt

Matthew 2:1–23

I'm tired. Bed is going to feel good tonight, Joseph thought. But just a few hours later something strange happened.

"Joseph, wake up. I have a message for you. It's from God," a voice said. An angel stood in front of him.

"I know you. You came to me once before and told me Mary was going to have a baby who was the Son of God," Joseph whispered.

"That's right. I am an angel sent by God. He wants you to take Mary and Jesus and leave Bethlehem," the angel said.

"But why?" Joseph asked; he was confused by the command.

"King Herod wants to get rid of Jesus. He is jealous that Jesus is called the King of the Jews. You have to leave now. Take your family and go to Egypt. I'll tell you when it's safe to come home," the angel said.

Joseph woke Mary. "Get up. We have to leave town now!" As they disappeared into the darkness, Joseph explained what the angel had told him.

The little family arrived safely in Egypt. "Jesus is safe, and that's the most important thing," Joseph reminded Mary when she got discouraged. She missed her friends.

A few years later, the angel came again and said to Joseph, "It's safe to go home now. King Herod is dead." Mary and Joseph happily returned to their hometown, Nazareth.

Becoming a Woman of God

A woman of God protects.

Joseph followed the instructions the angel gave him to protect Jesus.

When has your mom or dad protected you from danger? Did it feel good to know they were taking care of you?

A Verse to Remember

The LORD guards you as you come and go, now and forever.

Psalm 121:8

The Temptation of Jesus

Matthew 4:1–11

Not long after being baptized by John the Baptist, Jesus left everyone he knew. He went out to the wilderness by himself.

For forty days and forty nights Jesus sat alone in the wilderness. He had no food and nothing to drink. The only person who came to be with him was his biggest enemy, Satan.

"Are you hungry, Jesus? You're the Son of God—why don't you turn these stones into bread?" Satan snarled, tossing a handful of stones at Jesus's feet.

"The Scriptures say that people need more than bread for life. They need to feed on the Word of God," Jesus answered, as he turned his back on Satan.

Satan whisked Jesus to the highest point at the top of the temple. "If you're really the Son of God, jump off," he challenged. "The Bible says that God will send his angels to keep you from being hurt."

"The Bible says not to test the Lord," Jesus answered.

Then Satan took Jesus to the top of a tall mountain. "Look at all the nations of the world. See their glory and riches? They can all be yours. Just bow down and worship me," Satan said.

"Go away," Jesus said. "The Scriptures say to worship only God."

Then Satan left.

Becoming a Woman of God

A woman of God fights temptation.

Jesus knows what it's like when we're tempted to do something wrong. Satan tempted him three times, and Jesus answered each temptation with a verse of Scripture.

How do you fight temptation?

A Verse to Remember

Your word is a lamp for my feet
and a light for my path.

Psalm 119:105

The Beginning
John 2:1-11

Mary was excited to see Jesus at the wedding celebration. She enjoyed seeing old friends and catching up.

"Isn't the bride beautiful?" Mary said to a friend. The whole event was wonderful. Then Mary heard that the master of ceremonies was worrying about something. *Oh dear,* she thought. *I hate for anything to spoil this special day. I know Jesus can help.* She saw Jesus and ran to him. "The party isn't over, but they've run out of wine," she told him.

"I can't help them. It's not time for me to do miracles yet," Jesus said.

Turning to the servants, Mary said, "Do whatever Jesus tells you to do."

Jesus looked at his mother for a long time then said to the servants, "Fill six big jars with water."

They filled the jars and brought them to Jesus. He didn't even touch the jars, but just said, "Dip some out and take it to the master of ceremonies."

Mary heard the man say, "This is the best wine I've ever tasted!" The servants were amazed. They knew they had put water in those jars—not wine.

Mary knew this was just the first of many miracles Jesus would do. His disciples knew Jesus wasn't just an ordinary man. He was the Son of God. Mary thought, *Soon everyone will know that Jesus is God's own Son.*

Becoming a Woman of God

*A woman of God recognizes
Jesus's power.*

Mary knew who Jesus was. She believed in his power and expected him to help people who needed his help. Jesus saw how much faith she had and he did his first miracle at this wedding.

It's a good thing to see Jesus's power. Expecting him to help you when you need it is called faith.

A Verse to Remember

When you ask for something, don't have any doubts. A person who has doubts is like a wave that is blown by the wind and tossed by the sea.

James 1:6

Just a Word

Matthew 8:5–13

"Sir, I polished your shield last night," the servant said as he leaned the shiny shield against the wall.

"Thank you," the Roman officer said.

The servant bowed as he left the room. He was happy to serve the officer. The officer was an important man in the Roman army, and he had many servants.

A few days later the officer was working at his desk when another servant dashed into the room. "Sir, one of your servants is very sick." The officer ran to the servant's quarters and found his special servant lying in bed in terrible pain.

The Roman officer didn't know what to do to help his servant. Then he remembered hearing that Jesus was in town. "He heals sick people using the power of God," he said. Grabbing his helmet, he ran into town.

"Sir, my servant is very sick," the officer told Jesus.

"I'll come and heal him," Jesus said.

"That's not necessary. If you just say the word, I know he will be healed," the officer said.

Jesus couldn't believe what he was hearing. "I haven't seen this kind of faith before," he said to his followers. "Go home," he told the officer. "Your servant has been healed."

Becoming a Woman of God

A woman of God helps others.

The officer had faith that Jesus could just say the words and the servant would be healed.

How big is your faith? When you ask God to do something, do you really truly believe he will do it?

A Verse to Remember

Judge me favorably, O LORD,
　　because I have walked with integrity
　　　　and I have trusted you without wavering.

Psalm 26:1

Getting Out of the Boat

Matthew 14:22–33

Peter settled down in the boat just as it lurched sideways.

"This storm is getting so bad that the boat is bouncing all over," Andrew said.

"We all need to help if we're going to keep ourselves out of the water," John shouted over the wind.

"I wish Jesus was here," someone said. "Things are always okay when he's with us."

"Well, he's not, and we're in trouble here!" Peter shouted.

All the disciples were frightened. One of them said,
"Look over there. Do you see something?"

Peter stared through the waves. "It looks like a man.
How could a man be walking around on the water, in
a storm?"

"It's me! Don't be afraid; I'm coming to help you," a voice called.

"Jesus?" Peter leaned out to get a better look. "Jesus, is that you? If it is, let me come to you."

Jesus said, "Yes, Peter, come to me."

In a split second Peter was out of the boat and walking across the water. "I'm coming, Jesus," he called. When Peter realized he was walking on water, he began to sink. "H-e-l-p m-e!" he cried.

As Jesus helped Peter into the boat, the wind stopped blowing. Jesus said, "Didn't you trust me to keep you safe?"

Becoming a Woman of God

A woman of God gets out of the boat.

Peter wanted to be with Jesus so badly that he hopped out of the boat when Jesus called him. Peter would have been OK if he had just kept his eyes on Jesus and not looked at the waves. For just an instant, Peter showed awesome faith, the kind of faith that can do exciting things for God.

A Verse to Remember

The LORD is my light and my salvation.
    Who is there to fear?
The LORD is my life's fortress.
    Who is there to be afraid of?

Psalm 27:1

Forgive and Forget

Matthew 18:23–35

A king decided to collect debts that were owed to him. One man owed him millions of dollars.

"Pay me back. Otherwise, you, your wife, and your children will be sold as slaves," the king told the man. The poor man was scared.

"Please have mercy on me. I'll pay it all back, I promise. Just give me some time," he begged. The king had a soft heart, so he released the family and completely forgave the debt. The man didn't have to pay it back.

As the man was walking home, he saw another man
who owed him a few hundred dollars. "I want my money
now!" he yelled as he grabbed the man by the collar.

The poor man begged, "Just give me some time and I'll get the money. I promise."

"No. You're going to jail," the angry man shouted. Some of the king's servants saw the whole thing. They knew that the king had forgiven the first man's debt, which was much bigger than the second man's debt.

The servants ran to the king and told him what had happened. He was angry. The king had the first man thrown into jail until he could pay back the millions of dollars he owed. "I forgave your big debt. You should have forgiven the other man's debt too," the king said.

Jesus told this story to teach us about forgiving people because God forgives us.

Becoming a Woman of God

A woman of God is fair.

The king generously forgave the huge debt that one man owed him. The man should have done the same thing for the man who owed him money. But he didn't.

Is there someone you need to forgive?

A Verse to Remember

Always do for other people everything you want them to do for you.

Matthew 7:12

Your Money or Your Life!

Matthew 19:16–24

The young man rode down the street in his fancy carriage. He liked it when people noticed him. *They must think that I am important because I have so much money,* he thought.

One day as the rich man was riding through town, he saw a crowd of people sitting under a tree listening to a man teach. He got out of his carriage and walked over to the crowd. His gold jewelry jingled as he walked, and he didn't try to keep it quiet.

"Shhhh!" someone said. "We're trying to hear what Jesus says."

The rich man listened to Jesus teaching about eternal life. *I wonder what that costs*, he thought. When Jesus was finished speaking, the rich man asked him, "What do I have to do to get eternal life?" He jingled the gold in his pocket, thinking that he might be able to buy it.

"There's only one way—obey the commandments," Jesus replied.

"Which ones?" the rich man asked.

Jesus answered, "Don't murder, steal, or lie. Honor your father and mother and love your neighbor as much as you love yourself."

"No problem," said the rich man. "I've done all those."

"Then," Jesus continued, "sell everything you own and give the money to the poor." The rich man was shocked. He shook his head and walked away. He loved his stuff too much to obey Jesus.

Becoming a Woman of God

*A woman of God keeps God
most important.*

The rich man really liked being rich. He didn't want God to have first place in his life; he wanted to be in control himself.

Is there something that's more important to you than God?

A Verse to Remember

Love the LORD your God with all your heart, with all your soul, and with all your strength.

Deuteronomy 6:5

Following Through

Matthew 21:28–32

"Why do we have to spend all our time working?" one boy asked, as he swept the floor.

"Yeah, there will be plenty of time to work when we're grown up," his brother answered, putting a plate in the cupboard.

Just then their father came in. "Will you pick grapes in the vineyard this afternoon?" he asked his oldest son.

"No. All I do is work. I'm tired of it," the boy said as he stomped out of the house.

"How about you? Will you help in the vineyards?" the father asked his younger boy.

"I guess so," the boy said. He wasn't excited about it, but he didn't want to argue.

Then he started playing with his puppy and forgot all about working in the vineyard.

When his father came home, he said, "Son, you said you'd pick grapes for me today, but you didn't do it. Now I'm going to have to work overtime to get the work done." He wasn't very happy with his younger son.

The father was tired and disappointed. But when he got to the vineyard, he saw something that surprised him.

There was his older son—picking grapes—the same work he had said he wouldn't do.

"Thank you," the father said. "I am so glad you changed your mind. Your brother said he would help, but he didn't. I thought he was the obedient son, but it really is you because you are doing the work."

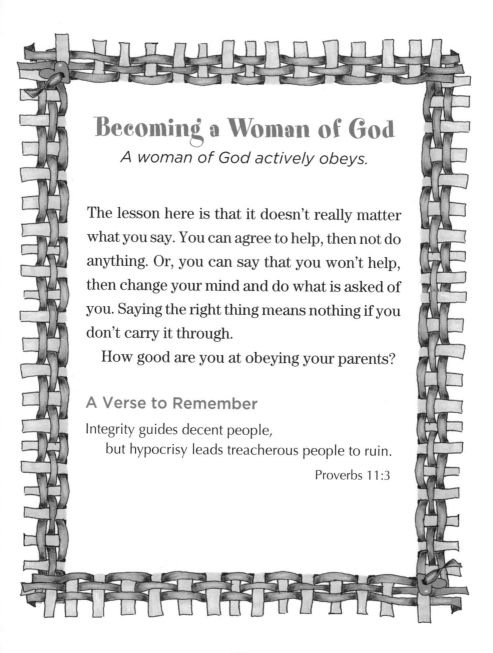

Becoming a Woman of God

A woman of God actively obeys.

The lesson here is that it doesn't really matter what you say. You can agree to help, then not do anything. Or, you can say that you won't help, then change your mind and do what is asked of you. Saying the right thing means nothing if you don't carry it through.

How good are you at obeying your parents?

A Verse to Remember

Integrity guides decent people,
but hypocrisy leads treacherous people to ruin.

Proverbs 11:3

191

Ninety-Nine and Counting

Luke 15:1–7

The shepherd led his flock to a field filled with sweet green grass. While the sheep ate breakfast, he settled down under a tree and watched for any animals that might attack his flock.

One little lamb wandered farther and farther from the herd. The shepherd thought, *I'm always shooing him back into the flock. Why can't he stay with the group like the others?* But he gently led the lamb back to the flock.

After the sheep finished eating, the shepherd settled
back against the tree, but he didn't go to sleep because
he had to protect his flock.

Later in the afternoon the shepherd stood up and stretched. He called his sheep to follow him, and they recognized his voice. He climbed up on a big rock and counted the sheep. "One, two, three . . ." He knew every sheep in his flock. "Ninety-seven, ninety-eight, ninety-nine . . ." That wasn't right. Where was the 100th sheep?

The one missing is that little lamb. Where could he be? The shepherd left the ninety-nine sheep alone and ran to find the missing lamb. It didn't matter that he still had ninety-nine sheep or that the missing one was always wandering off. The shepherd searched until he found the little lamb and brought him safely back to the flock.

Becoming a Woman of God

A woman of God knows she is special to him.

The shepherd had ninety-nine sheep left. Why did he care if one little sheep wandered away? Why didn't he just let it go? Because every single sheep was important to the shepherd. This story reminds us that every single person is important to God too.

A Verse to Remember

Lead me in your truth and teach me
    because you are God, my savior.
    I wait all day long for you.

Psalm 25:5

The Last Chance

Mark 5:25–34

I know he can help me. I have nothing to lose, the woman thought. She had been sick for a long time and tried every cure suggested. Nothing helped. She thought Jesus could help.

The woman pushed her way through the crowd behind Jesus. Bending down low, she touched the hem of his robe. Her faith in him was so strong that she believed this simple touch could heal her. As her fingers brushed the fabric, she felt her sickness leave her.

She heard Jesus ask, "Who touched me?" His disciples tried to ignore him. After all, people were pushing against him on every side.

The woman felt as if Jesus was looking right at her. "Someone touched me. I felt power leave me," Jesus said.

She wanted to turn and run, but she couldn't. "I touched you," she said. "I've been sick so long. I just wanted to be well and I knew that touching you would heal me," she said, not daring to look up.

When I touched your robe, I was healed....

Everyone waited to hear what Jesus would say, but he asked the woman to continue. "When I touched your robe, I felt something. I think I'm well," she said. A ripple of shock rolled through the crowd.

Jesus smiled gently before saying, "Your faith made you well. Go in peace."

Becoming a Woman of God

A woman of God takes a chance.

This woman had such strong faith that she believed just touching Jesus's clothing would help her.

Faith means that you believe something is true even if you can't actually see it. That kind of belief gives you the strength to take a chance.

A Verse to Remember

My God will richly fill your every need in a glorious way through Christ Jesus.

Philippians 4:19

A Miracle Touch

Mark 5:22-24, 35-43

The little girl adored her daddy, Jairus, and believed he could do anything. Then something terrible happened— the little girl got very sick. For the first time in her life, something happened that Jairus couldn't fix.

"Don't worry," her dad said. "I'm going to find someone who can help you. I'll be back soon." Jairus had heard about a man named Jesus who healed sick people in God's name. He was determined to get Jesus to help his precious daughter.

The little girl waited and waited, getting weaker every day. Her momma stayed with her and prayed every day for her daughter to get better. The little girl tried to hang on. But before her daddy could come back, she died.

The heartbroken mother sent a servant to tell her husband not to bother Jesus. "Your little girl is dead," the servant whispered gently. Sadly, Jairus turned to go home. Then he felt a hand on his arm. "I'm coming with you," Jesus said.

Jesus went into the house. "Why are you crying?" he asked the crowd of people. "She's not dead, just sleeping." Jesus sent everyone away except Jairus and his wife. Then he took the little girl's hand and said, "Get up, little girl." *And she did!* Jesus brought her back to life by the power of God.

Becoming a Woman of God

*A woman of God thanks God
for second chances.*

Jairus's daughter got a second chance at life.
Don't you think she felt special when her dad
told her the story of Jesus bringing her back to
life? She knew that her dad loved her and Jesus
loved her.

Have you ever gotten a second chance at
something? God gives us second chances when
we confess our sins.

A Verse to Remember

I made my sins known to you, and I did not cover
up my guilt.
I decided to confess them to you, O LORD.
Then you forgave all my sins.

Psalm 32:5

Giving from
the Heart

Mark 12:41–44

The old woman peeked out from behind a pillar, waiting for her turn to give her offering. "Praise you, God," she prayed. "Thank you for everything you have given me."

The woman was very poor and she never knew where her next meal was coming from. Her husband was dead and she didn't have family.

The woman held the bag containing two small coins tightly in her hand as she stood in line.

A rich man stepped up to the offering box ahead of her. He made a big show of dropping gold coins in the box as he loudly prayed, "O God, you are very lucky to have a man like me paying attention to you." The man made sure everyone in the temple noticed him.

When it was her turn, the widow dropped her two coins into the offering box. They were barely worth a penny together, but her heart was filled with praise to God. The rich man exploded in laughter. "That offering isn't even worth the space it takes up in the box," he said.

The old woman didn't hear him though. She was busy praying that God would use her offering to help people who were poorer than she was. The woman looked up and saw Jesus watching her. He knew that this poor woman had given everything she had to God's work, while the rich man only gave his extra money to God.

Becoming a Woman of God

A woman of God is humble.

This woman didn't hold anything back from God. She was also very humble. The rich man ahead of her was more concerned with having everyone know how important he was.

Do you know anyone who is always bragging about how smart they are or how good they are at something? Do you enjoy being around a person like that?

A Verse to Remember

Don't act out of selfish ambition or be conceited. Instead, humbly think of others as being better than yourselves.

Philippians 2:3

A Surprise Friend

Luke 10:30–37

A man was enjoying his walk to Jericho, until two men jumped on him and beat him up. They took his money and his clothes.

The man moaned, "Who will help me?" Then he heard footsteps. *Oh good, it's a priest. I'm sure he will help me,* he thought. But the priest crossed the road and kept walking.

The sun was straight overhead when the man heard footsteps again. He strained to see who was coming. "A temple worker. Help me, please!" he whispered.

"You're in bad shape," the temple worker said, "but I have to get to work." He stepped over the man and kept walking.

It was nearly dark before the man heard someone else coming by. This time he didn't make a sound. He had given up on anyone helping him. But then, he felt someone gently lift his head and slide a pillow underneath. *This has to be a dream*, he thought as he peeked through one eye. *Why would this Samaritan help me?*

The man woke up later in a nice clean bed. His cuts were clean and bandaged. The Samaritan was asking the innkeeper to take care of the hurt man. He even paid the innkeeper. *I am so thankful for the kindness of the Samaritan. When I get better I will help others like he helped me,* the man thought.

Becoming a Woman of God

A woman of God helps others.

The priest and temple worker in this story did not help the man who was hurt even though they all lived in the same area. The Samaritan was from a different region, but he was kind to the hurt man anyway. Sometimes people who need our help—or who help us—may be different from us.

Do you know any people who are different from you?

A Verse to Remember

I'm giving you a new commandment: Love each other in the same way that I have loved you.

John 13:34

What's Most Important?

Luke 10:38–42

Mary and Martha were as different as two sisters could be. Martha was a "doer" and Mary was a "dreamer."

Mary loved long walks, smelling flowers, and sitting for hours talking to people. Martha was always busy working in the house or the yard. She couldn't sit still. She always saw something that needed to be done.

Today Martha was cooking and baking. She wanted to serve Jesus a wonderful dinner. She thought, *It sure would be nice if Mary helped a little.*

When Jesus came in, Mary sat down to listen to him. Martha listened for a few minutes but then hurried to the kitchen to finish dinner. She thought Mary would help her in a few minutes, but she didn't.

Martha rushed around the kitchen. Every few minutes she peeked out to see if Mary was coming. She wasn't. In fact, every time Martha looked, Mary and Jesus seemed to be having more fun than the last time. Pretty soon Martha was angry. *Why do I have to do all the work around here?* she thought.

Marching into the other room, Martha said to Jesus, "Tell Mary to get up and help me. I'd like to hear your stories too, but someone has to make dinner!"

Jesus was surprised at Martha's anger. Jesus gently said, "Martha, you work so hard. I really appreciate it, but I'd rather just have you make a simple meal so we can spend more time together."

Becoming a Woman of God

*A woman of God
wants to spend time with Jesus.*

Martha meant well. She wanted to have a nice house and good food to serve her guests. The problem was that her housework became more important than the people she was serving. Nothing should be more important than spending time with Jesus.

A Verse to Remember

I will thank the LORD at all times.
My mouth will always praise him.

Psalm 34:1

A Father's Love

Luke 15:11–32

"Plant the seed. Hoe the field. Mend the fences. I don't want to do this anymore," the young man said. "There must be more to life than this. I want to go to a country far away from home and have some fun."

The young man ran into the barn. "Hey, Dad, give me my share of your money now," he said. When his son took the money and headed for a faraway country, the old man watched sadly.

Once he was there, the young man was surrounded by friends who enjoyed helping him spend his money. But then he ran out of money and suddenly all his "friends" were gone.

"I can't believe that none of my friends will help me. I paid for everything for them before my money ran out. Now, the only job I can get is feeding pigs. The pigs have more to eat than I do," he said to himself. Meanwhile, his dad kept watching for him to come home.

As the young man walked home, he came up with a plan. "I need to tell my dad that I am sorry. I'll just ask him for a job because I don't deserve to be called his son anymore." The young man was surprised when his dad ran out to meet him and hugged him tight. His father was ready to forgive him and celebrated his return home.

Becoming a Woman of God

A woman of God never gives up hope.

The dad loved his son very much and never gave up hope that the boy would come home. When the boy came back and said he was sorry, everything he had done was forgiven.

This story is an example of how much God loves you. He wants his children to live for him and stay close to him. He completely forgives you even when you do not deserve it.

A Verse to Remember

Love never stops being patient, never stops believing, never stops hoping, never gives up.

1 Corinthians 13:7

Forgotten Thanks

Luke 17:11–19

"Having leprosy means I can't even see my family. I have to live in this leper colony," a man said.

"I know," another man said. "I wish I could just hug my kids."

Jesus passed by the leper colony on his way to Jerusalem. "Jesus, please help us," one man called. Jesus looked around and saw ten men standing near some trees. Their heads and hands were wrapped in strips of cloth because they had leprosy, a skin disease.

Jesus walked toward the lepers even though other people were backing away from them. "Go into town and show yourself to the priest," he told them.

People in the crowd whispered, "Did you hear that? He told them to go into town. They can't do that; they're lepers. Someone might catch the disease from them."

The ten men took off running toward the nearby town. "Look at my hands. The white leprosy spots are fading!" one man called to the others.

All ten men stopped to check their own hands, arms, and faces. "My leprosy is gone too. Jesus healed me," each man said.

Nine men ran for their homes and families. But one man turned around and went back to Jesus. He dropped to the ground, his face near Jesus's feet. "Thank you so much for healing me," he said.

"You're welcome," Jesus answered. "But where are the other nine? Didn't I heal ten men?"

Becoming a Woman of God

A woman of God says thank you.

Jesus healed ten lepers, but only one took the time to say thank you. How do you think that made Jesus feel?

Do you remember to say thank you when someone does something for you? How do you feel when you do something for another person and they don't thank you?

A Verse to Remember

Give thanks to the LORD.
Call on his name.
Make known among the nations what he has done.

1 Chronicles 16:8

Keep On Asking!

Luke 18:1–8

The woman looked helpless as her landlord walked away, counting the money he had just cheated her out of. "How long are you going to let him cheat you?" her neighbor asked. "If you don't do something, all the money your husband left you will be gone."

She knew that her neighbor was right. The only thing she could think to do was to go see the local judge. Even though she'd heard he was unkind, she thought he might help her.

The woman took a deep breath before marching up to the judge. "Will you please stop my landlord from cheating me? I'm a widow and I don't have much money," she explained. The judge stared at her.

"Get out of here. I can't be bothered with such minor problems," he said.

Turning to leave, the woman thought, *What do I have to lose? If he doesn't help me I'm going to lose everything anyway.* So she marched right back to the judge and said, "Sir, you are the only one who can help me. Please listen to my story." But the judge told her to leave.

However, the widow did not give up easily. Time after time, she went back to the judge and respectfully asked him to help her. Time after time, he sent her away, but she kept on going back. Finally he said, "You're wearing me out. I'm going to see that you get the help you need because you just keep asking me."

244

Becoming a Woman of God

A woman of God is persistent in prayer.

The woman could have asked the judge for help one time, then given up. But what she wanted was important to her, so she kept asking. Finally, the judge gave her what she wanted.

Keep asking God for what you want. Let him know how important things are to you.

A Verse to Remember

Ask, and you will receive. Search, and you will find. Knock, and the door will be opened for you.

Matthew 7:7

Bird's-Eye View

Luke 19:1–10

"Out of my way; let me through," the tough little man said. But no one paid any attention to him.

Crowds of people swarmed the streets. A tax collector like Zacchaeus, who cheated and overcharged people, had no chance of anyone letting him move to the front. Everyone wanted to see Jesus.

Meanwhile, little Zacchaeus had an idea. A big sycamore tree grew nearby. One of its branches hung out over the crowd of people. So Zacchaeus climbed up the tree and scooted out to the end of the branch. Now he was hanging right over the road where Jesus would pass.

A few minutes later Jesus and a crowd of people appeared down the road. As they moved toward the tree, cries of "Jesus, look at me; Jesus, over here; Jesus, heal my friend" filled the air. Zacchaeus just sat quietly on his tree branch and watched the whole thing.

As Jesus passed under the tree branch, he looked up at Zacchaeus. "Come on down, Zacchaeus. I want to come to your house today," he said.

"Why would Jesus go to a tax collector's house?" people asked.

After Zacchaeus talked with Jesus for a while, he knew it had been wrong to cheat people. He promised Jesus he would pay back everyone he had cheated.

Becoming a Woman of God

*A woman of God changes
when she meets Jesus.*

Zacchaeus cheated others. He thought he was
more important than others. But when Jesus
talked to him and told him about God's love,
Zacchaeus changed. He was sorry for the way he
had cheated people and wanted to change. That
is the effect Jesus has on people. How have you
changed since coming to know Jesus?

A Verse to Remember

God loved the world this way: He gave his only Son
so that everyone who believes in him will not die but
will have eternal life.

John 3:16

My Son, My Savior
John 19:1–30

Mary knew what the Scripture taught about the Messiah. He would save people from their sins. She remembered the angel telling her that she was going to have a baby—Jesus—who was God's Son, the Messiah. She had watched Jesus grow into a strong young man. She saw him do miracles and heard him tell people how much God loved them.

But now, Jesus was going to die. Mary watched Jesus drag the wooden cross on which he would die. "*No!*" she wanted to scream at the soldiers. "You can't do this! He's my son and I love him. He's God's Son. Please, stop this!" But as painful as it was, she knew this was God's plan.

She followed Jesus to a place called Golgotha. When
the soldiers nailed his hands and feet to the cross, Mary
couldn't bear to watch.

The soldiers dropped the cross into the ground, and Mary crept up close to it. She looked into Jesus's eyes, which were filled with love, even for those who had done this horrible thing to him.

When Jesus died, Mary dropped to her knees, sobbing in pain. "My son. They've killed my son," she cried. God quietly spoke to her heart. "They've killed *my* Son," he seemed to say. "This was my plan to save a sinful world."

Becoming a Woman of God

*A woman of God understands
Jesus's sacrifice.*

The day Jesus died was a terrible day for his friends and especially for his mother. They knew he had never done anything wrong. Jesus could have called thousands of angels to rescue him from the cross, but he didn't. He died so that we could someday live in heaven with him.

A Verse to Remember

Believe in the Lord Jesus, and you and your family will be saved.

Acts 16:31

A New Beginning

Luke 24:1-12

Early Sunday morning, three women headed to Jesus's tomb. "I can't believe he's dead," one of them said.

The women carried baskets filled with spices and perfumes. Their custom was to put these on the bodies of those who had died. They couldn't do it the day Jesus died, because the Sabbath came and no work was permitted. So they agreed to meet early the next morning.

"What about the stone?" one woman suddenly asked. The other two stopped so quickly that they nearly spilled the spices from their baskets. "How are we going to move the huge stone that is in front of the tomb? It took several men just to roll it in place."

"We'll figure something out," one of the women replied.

As they came near the tomb, one woman shouted, "The stone is gone!" All three women stared at the open tomb, trying to figure out what this meant, when an angel stepped through the door. "I know you're looking for Jesus," the angel said. "He isn't here. He came back to life, just as he said he would."

For just a moment the women seemed unable to believe what had happened. Then they exploded in joy. "Jesus is alive!" Jumping and shouting, the three women ran to tell the rest of Jesus's friends. "He's alive; our Savior is alive!"

Becoming a Woman of God

A woman of God celebrates.

The women must have been heartbroken when Jesus died. When they saw the open tomb and the angel said Jesus was alive, their hearts must have leaped into their throats. They went from being very sad to very happy.

A Verse to Remember

You are my hope, O Almighty LORD.
You have been my confidence ever since I was young.

Psalm 71:5

What Could Be Better than Money?

Acts 3:1–10

"Hurry, John, the prayer service will be starting soon," Peter said. John quickly finished the rest of his lunch as he followed Peter out the door. The temple wasn't far away, but the streets were crowded.

Some men were trying to get through the crowd. They were carrying a man who couldn't walk.

"They bring him here every day to beg for money," Peter said. He and John watched as the man settled down near the temple gate and started begging.

Peter walked over to the crippled man and stood in front of him. The man held up his cup, expecting Peter to drop some money in it. "I don't have any money," Peter said. "I have something better for you than money."

The man didn't look so sure. What could be better than money?

"Come on, we're going to be late for prayers," John said, tugging at Peter's sleeve. Peter shook him away and turned back to the man.

"In the name of Jesus, get up and walk," he said.

Peter took the man's hand and helped him to his feet. At first the man didn't understand what had happened; then he realized that his feet and legs were healed. Carefully, he took a step, then a hop; finally he was jumping and shouting, "I'm healed; praise God!"

Becoming a Woman of God

A woman of God gives the best gifts.

The crippled man thought that the best gift he could get was money. But Peter knew better. He knew that God would help him heal the man. Have you ever been able to help someone? How did it feel?

A Verse to Remember

The payment for sin is death, but the gift that God freely gives is everlasting life found in Christ Jesus our Lord.

Romans 6:23

Yours, Mine, and Ours

Acts 4:32–37

"Why do we always have to meet secretly?" a young man asked. Life had been hard for Jesus's followers since he returned to heaven.

"Don't get discouraged. We all miss Jesus, but we have to stay together and try to help each other," the disciples said.

"I'm sorry, I know that God will take care of us. It's just hard sometimes," the young man said. "How will I feed my family?"

Barnabas stepped up to the young man and put his arms around him. "The most important thing is for us to tell others that Jesus died because he loves them and that he came back to life and lives in heaven today. You can't do that if you're hungry or worried. Here, I sold some of my land and I want you to have this money."

"I have extra flour and oil," one old woman told the disciples. "If anyone needs some to make bread for their family, I'll give them some."

Another man mentioned that he had milk to share. A young woman had chickens who laid lots of eggs. Everyone helped others.

No one in the little church went hungry. If one person needed money, someone else sold a field and donated the money. If someone needed help, people volunteered to do what they could. The Christians shared God's love with others. People in the town could see how much they cared for each other. The Christians were good examples of God's love.

Becoming a Woman of God

A woman of God shares.

The Christians in the early church took care of one another. That's the way we should help one another today.

If you have two blankets and someone else doesn't have any, should you put your extra blanket in a closet or give it to the other person? Has another person shared something with you? Have you been able to share with another person?

A Verse to Remember

Whoever is generous will be blessed
   because he has shared his food with the poor.

Proverbs 22:9

Singin', Shakin', and Savin'

Acts 16:16–34

In the city of Philippi, people complained that Paul and Silas were troublemakers. They threw sticks at them and dragged them away to prison.

"You won't escape from here," the jailer said as he pushed Paul and Silas to the floor in the smallest cell of the jail.

Paul and Silas started praying and singing praises to God. "What do you have to sing about? Haven't you noticed that you're in prison?" the other prisoners asked Paul and Silas.

The other prisoners seemed to be comforted by Paul and Silas's singing. Around midnight the floor began to shake, and pieces of the ceiling dropped down on the prisoners. As the doors broke off and chains popped loose, men shouted, "We're free; run!"

But Paul didn't let anyone leave. When the jailer ran in and saw the doors were broken off, he cried, "My prisoners have all escaped."

"Don't panic. We're all here," Paul shouted.

The jailer was amazed. "Can you tell me how to be a Christian like you?" he asked. Paul was happy to do just that.

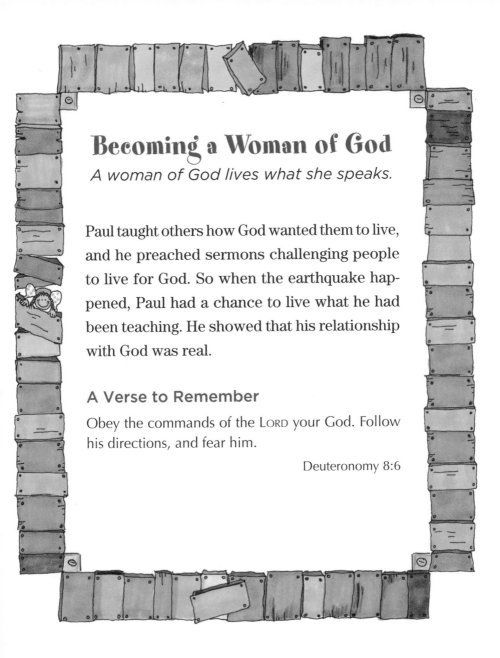

Becoming a Woman of God

A woman of God lives what she speaks.

Paul taught others how God wanted them to live, and he preached sermons challenging people to live for God. So when the earthquake happened, Paul had a chance to live what he had been teaching. He showed that his relationship with God was real.

A Verse to Remember

Obey the commands of the LORD your God. Follow his directions, and fear him.

Deuteronomy 8:6

Eavesdropping

Acts 23:12-35

"Uncle Paul, I'm scared. Why did those men put you in prison?" Paul's nephew asked. He visited him at the jail every day.

"They're angry because I teach about God," Paul answered. "It will be OK. Go on home and get some rest," Paul encouraged his young nephew.

After saying good-bye, the boy rounded a corner and heard men's voices. They sounded angry. He quietly listened for a few minutes. He couldn't believe what he heard.

Racing back to the prison, he called, "Uncle Paul, some men are going to trick the commander into bringing you to the High Council for questioning. Only, they're going to kidnap you instead."

"Shhhh, keep your voice down," Paul whispered. "Are you sure about this?"

When the young boy nodded his head, Paul said, "OK, here's what we'll do. I'll call the main officer over here and you tell him what you just told me. You are sure, aren't you?"

"Yeah, the men even said that they wouldn't eat anything until they got rid of you!"

The brave boy did exactly what Paul told him to do. Quickly the officer arranged for 200 soldiers, 200 spearmen, and 70 horsemen to get Paul safely out of town. Paul gave his nephew a big hug before leaving. "You saved my life," he told him.

Becoming a Woman of God

A woman of God tells an adult.

When Paul's nephew heard what the men were planning, he told Paul about it. That took courage. Sometimes we may know when there is a problem, but we don't know what to do about it. It's a good idea to tell someone you can trust.

Have you ever told an adult about some problem you have or that you have heard about?

A Verse to Remember

Train a child in the way he should go,
    and even when he is old he will not turn away
    from it.

Proverbs 22:6

Bible Storybooks for the
Whole Family

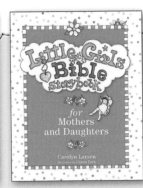

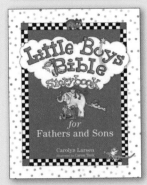

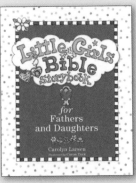

  Available wherever books and ebooks are sold.